FROM THE HEART

Written by Marla Daley

Copyright © 2024 by Marla Daley

"To trust Him means, of course, trying to do all that He says. There would be no sense in saying you trusted a person if you would not take his advice. Thus if you have really handed yourself over to Him, it must follow that you are trying to obey Him. But trying in a new way, a less worried way. Not doing these things in order to be saved, but because He has begun to save you already. Not hoping to get to Heaven as a reward for your actions, but inevitably wanting to act in a certain way because a first faint gleam of Heaven is already inside you."

— C.S. Lewis, Mere Christianity

How to use this study

This study is designed for children ages 13+ and is structured in such a way that it gradually expands on different dimensions of obedience each day.
It is recommended that you allow your child to complete the study independently. You can then review their daily work, discuss any talking points, and provide additional guidance as necessary. Bible verses referenced use the NIV translation.

Scripture memorization

Throughout this study, your child will discover the importance of God's Word in guiding His children to obey Him. They will also learn the value of memorizing Bible verses as a useful tool. Each week, your child will focus on memorizing a new verse related to obedience. The corresponding memory verses for each week can be found on pages 61-70. After completing the daily study pages, encourage your child to go to the listed memory verse page, read the verse aloud multiple times, and then copy it onto the page provided. At the end of each week, test your child's ability to recite the memory verse. Keep testing them weekly to confirm they have memorized not just the current week's verse, but also still recall the verses from the previous weeks. By the end of the 6-week study, your child should be able to share all 6 verses with you from memory.

Prayer

Each day of this study concludes with a short recommended prayer reflecting on the lesson learned. It's important to motivate your child to sincerely engage in prayer and guide them on how to expand upon the suggested prayer. This is a valuable opportunity for them to communicate with God and ask for His help with their struggles.

CONTENTS

Week 4

Day 16: Give yourself completely

Day 17: Our Obedience Is Our Witness

Day 18: The Blessings of Obedience

Day 19: Why is Obedience Important?

Day 20: Don't Let Pride Get in the Way

Week 5

Day 21: You're Going to Fail and That's ok

Day 22: Actions Speak Louder Than Words

Day 23: Consequences of Disobedience

Day 24: More Consequences of Disobedience

Day 25: Relationship Problems

Week 6

Day 26: Disobedience Hurts Our Witness

Day 27: God Gives us His Word

Day 28: God Gives us Prayer

Day 29: God's Tool: Suffering

Day 30: Obstacles to Obedience

Memory Verse Week 1

Memory Verse Week 2

Memory Verse Week 3

Memory Verse Week 4

Memory Verse Week 5

Memory Verse Week 6

BEFORE YOU BEGIN

Welcome to "From the Heart"! This book is designed specifically for young adults like you who are facing the many challenges of today's world while also striving to stay connected to God. Juggling school, activities, and friendships can be overwhelming, but by making time for God in your daily routine you can cultivate a deep and meaningful relationship with Him that will sustain you through life's challenges and uncertainties.

As you journey through the pages of this book you'll discover new insights into the significance of following God's guidance in your life. Each day presents powerful stories from the Bible paired with thought-provoking reflection questions. By studying the actions of biblical figures who have either listened to or disregarded God's guidance we can learn important lessons about the outcomes of our own choices. This also encourages us to reflect and consider whether our own decisions align with God's will for our lives. Ultimately, it's my hope that you will gain an understanding that God's commands are not about restricting your freedom but about guiding you toward a meaningful and purposeful life.

It's important to remember that the Bible is not just a book of stories, but a living, breathing guide for our lives. Before starting each lesson it's important to open your heart and mind to receive the wisdom and guidance that God has for you. Pray and ask Him to show you His truth and to help you understand what He wants you to learn. When you fully surrender yourself to God amazing things can happen. He can begin to change you from the inside out and transform your heart and mind. With that said, let's dive in!

CHRIST-LIKE CHARACTER

Together we're going to be studying the character trait of obedience so that we can grow into the image and likeness of Jesus. Character traits go hand-in-hand with the fruit of the Spirit, which are found in the Bible in the book of Galatians.

Read *Galatians 5:22-23* and list the 9 fruits of the Spirit.

_____   _____

_____   _____

_____   _____

_____   _____

_____

The fruits of the Spirit are the outward, visible, and godly qualities in a believer's life. These qualities point to the inward, invisible presence of the Holy Spirit. They are not good acts created out of our own strength, but the character traits that come from the Holy Spirit molding, shaping, and transforming us over time. The more deeply we grow in our relationship with God, the more these fruits become the obvious and noticeable result of that growth.

Growing spiritually can be compared to rolling out pizza dough. Both processes require patience, perseverance, and a willingness to adapt. This is a great example because if you squash pizza dough with a rolling pin it will try to snap back to its original shape. If you roll it out again it will snap back again, but this time it's a little bit wider. It can take a lot of tugging and rolling to get that pizza dough to finally conform to the pan. Similarly, our spiritual journey isn't always easy. We may encounter setbacks, doubts, and uncertainties. Sometimes it may even feel like we aren't growing at all. But, just like a pizza that needs time to rise and bake, our spiritual growth requires patience and faith. We must trust that God is guiding us, even when we can't see the bigger picture. As we grow spiritually, we start to follow Christ's teachings more closely, leading us to have more compassion, love, and understanding for others.

We learn to let go of our ego and embrace humility and forgiveness. Just as the sauce and toppings add flavor and depth to a pizza, the fruits of the Spirit – such as love, kindness, patience, and self-control – add richness and meaning to our lives. So, the next time you feel like you're facing challenges in your spiritual growth keep rolling out the dough, keep pushing forward, and keep adding the sauce and toppings. In the end, you're allowing God's love and grace to transform you with each passing day into a more compassionate, loving, and Christ-like individual.

Which fruits of the Spirit do you see showing up in your life most often? Give an example.

_____

_____

Which of the fruits of the Spirit do you struggle with most? List one way that you can intentionally display this fruit this week through your actions.

_____

_____

Living a life that reflects the character of Christ through our actions not only draws us nearer to God and strengthens our relationships with others, but it also has the potential to attract people to the message of Jesus. When we display these qualities, we become living proof of how His love can transform lives, serving as sources of light and hope in a world that is frequently overshadowed by darkness and despair.

Read **Matthew 5:16** and copy the verse below.

_____

_____

_____

We want to possess these Christ-like character traits because they allow us to honor God with the good fruit that grows in our lives!

During this study, you will be encouraged to connect with God through prayer and seek His guidance in your life. Take a moment to pray and ask God to help you stay humble, grow in your likeness to Christ, and provide you with chances to demonstrate your good fruit.

COMPLETE WEEK 1 MEMORY VERSE WORK ON PAGE 61

BE A DOER OF THE WORD

Obedience itself is not listed as a specific fruit of the Spirit in Galatians 5:22-23, but it's a necessary outcome of the Spirit's work in our lives. <u>Obedience is the result of our faith in God's grace and power</u>. Take a moment to really think about that. Because we believe and trust what the Bible says about God and His character, we have a desire to obey Him.

Yesterday we learned what it means to have godly character traits, but we need to make sure we don't stop there. Just knowing isn't enough; we want these traits to be present in our lives every day.

Read *James 1:22* and copy the verse below.

_____

_____

_____

James is warning us to not just know what God wants us to do but to make sure we act on it as well. **We need to be "doers" of the Word.**

Read *James 1:23-25*. Why do you think James compares God's Word to a mirror?

_____

_____

_____

Do you face any challenges in living out God's Word in certain areas of your life? Explain below.

_____

_____

_____

_____

James gives us the picture of a person who looks at their face in the mirror, rushes out the door, and forgets what they saw. Maybe this person's eyes are puffy from just waking up, and they slept wrong on their hair and it's unruly looking. They're really not at all concerned about their appearance, so they quickly try to rub their face, smooth out their hair, and rush out the door. The mirror showed them the problems, but they didn't do anything to fix them.

The Word of God is like a mirror that reveals to us the very thoughts and intentions of our hearts. It shows us our ugly, self-centered attitudes. It exposes our pride. It points out our sinful anger, our rotten speech, our deceitful nature, greed, and lack of compassion for others.

If we just take a quick glance at God's Word every once in a while and then rush out the door without doing anything to fix the problems that it reveals, it won't do us any good. Like Adam and Eve when God confronted them, we're quick to blame others and dodge our own responsibility for our sins. To be doers of the Word, we've got to give it more than just a passing glance. It requires careful focus and intentionality.

James' example isn't describing someone with a poor memory, but rather a person with poor priorities. This person doesn't remember what they saw in the mirror because they don't think of it as very important compared to the other things going on in their life.

Read **Luke 11:28** and fill in the blank below.

"Blessed rather are those who _____

_____ *."*

This is a promise that is given over and over again in the Bible. God's blessings are poured out on those who hear God's Word and obey it.

Pray and ask God to help you be a doer of His Word. Ask Him to open your eyes and help you to see your "problems in the mirror" and to give you the strength to correct them.

COMPLETE WEEK 1 MEMORY VERSE WORK ON PAGE 61

WHAT DOES OBEDIENCE REALLY MEAN?

The Bible provides countless stories that demonstrate how much God values obedience. What does the word obedience mean to you?

_____

_____

Read **Deuteronomy 28:1** and copy the verse below.

_____

_____

God is telling the Israelites that He expects them to fully obey His commands. Obedience is humbly submitting to God's authority and following His commandments. We are going to learn more each day during this study about how God wants us to obey. God shows us that it's not only the act of obeying a command but also the way in which we do so that shows obedience. Obedience is **quickly**, **joyfully**, **trustfully**, and **completely** doing what an authority asks of you. This also means doing what you know that authority would want even if you haven't been specifically told in that moment.

A good example of this is that I expect my children not to walk through the house with muddy shoes on. They have been asked enough times to understand that this is not something that I approve of or appreciate and that if they walk through the house and leave mud all over the floors they would be disobeying me even though I didn't just directly say it right at that moment. It's no longer an ongoing command, but it's **what is expected of you**.

Do you sometimes have a hard time obeying the rules that are expected of you at home? If so, explain below.

_____

_____

_____

Now it's time to sit down with Mom and Dad. Together, you will come up with a list of family expectations. This list should be clear and easy to understand.

A few examples of expectations could be:

- Obey Mom and Dad promptly when asked. We should not need to tell you more than once.
- You will be expected to follow directions without arguing or complaining.
- We will respect each other's personal space and privacy.
- As a family we will not yell when we get angry or frustrated, but we will have self-control instead.

FAMILY RULES

_____

_____

_____

_____

_____

_____

_____

_____

_____

_____

_____

_____

Pray and ask God for help to humbly obey and submit to your parents and to remember your family rules and obey them. Ask Him for help recognizing their authority over you and to let your obedience show love to them and Him and bring glory to His name.

COMPLETE WEEK 1 MEMORY VERSE WORK ON PAGE 61

OBEY QUICKLY

The Bible explains why it's important to listen to God and follow His rules. If you look closely, you'll notice it also teaches us *how* God wants us to obey. One key lesson that we learn about obedience is that God wants us to obey quickly. This means listening to what He asks of us and doing it right away. When you're a teenager, this can also mean listening to your parents and teachers promptly and respecting their guidance. By doing this, you're not only following God's teachings but also learning to make good choices that can help you in the future.

A good example of this is when I need to ask my kids for help with chores or to start their homework. Sometimes they get up to do what I asked right away. However, there are other times that they give me a half-hearted "okay", without really meaning it, and I notice that after several minutes they still haven't gotten up from what they were doing. When I check back in I may get the response "I'm going to right after this." This is where the disconnect occurs. They can't understand why I'm upset with them when they "were just about to go do it." They don't think they disobeyed; they just hadn't gotten around to obeying yet. Unfortunately, this isn't the case. Obedience that is not done right away is disobedience.

Read **Psalms 119:60** and copy the verse below.

_____

_____

When God tells you to do something, don't procrastinate. Don't make excuses. Don't drag your feet. Just do it.

Read **Jonah 1:1-3**. Where does God ask Jonah to go? Where did Jonah end up doing instead?

_____

_____

God said to Jonah, "Go to the great city of Ninevah", and what did Jonah do? He fled to Tarshish.

This was literally the exact opposite of what God wanted him to do. Tarshish was more than 2,500 miles from Israel in the opposite direction of Nineveh. It was the most remote destination available to Jonah. Jonah was clearly trying to put as much distance as he could between himself and Ninevah.

Jonah was just a regular guy who made mistakes like everyone else. We all have moments when we hear what God wants us to do but choose to do the opposite. You might already know how this story ends but if not you can check it out in Jonah chapters 1-3. Jonah couldn't outrun God and ended up obeying after a wild experience with a giant fish. We should aim to learn from Jonah's mistake and follow directions right away when God or an authority asks us to do something.

Take a moment to reflect on your life. Are there things you might be overlooking that God wants you to do? Is there anything that you're doing that goes against God's commands? Is there anything God has asked you to do that you haven't done yet?

_____

_____

_____

Do you always obey right away when your mom or dad asks you to do something? Do you ever give excuses as to why you can't or didn't do something right away?

_____

_____

Give an example of a recent situation that you were in where you didn't obey as quickly as you should have. How should you have handled the situation differently?

_____

_____

_____

Pray and ask God to help you to learn from Jonah and be obedient right away in the future. Ask for help to wholeheartedly surrender to Him without delay or hesitation.

COMPLETE WEEK 1 MEMORY VERSE WORK ON PAGE 62

OBEY ALL THE WAY

Have you ever been asked to put away a bunch of your things, but you only put away a few of them? Or have you ever washed your hands, as you were asked, but didn't use any soap? Do you think that obeying only part-way is acceptable? YES ○   ○ NO

Let's read about Moses today. Read **Numbers 20:2-8**. What did God ask Moses to do?

_____

_____

_____

Moses was a good leader and most of the time he did exactly what God asked him to do. Moses led the Israelites out of Egypt and into the desert, just as God had instructed him. Unfortunately, when they got to the Desert of Zin, the people started to complain that there was no good food and no water to drink. Moses and Aaron prayed and asked God what they should do. God promised Moses that if he gathered the people together and spoke to the rock, God would make water pour from the rock for the people to drink.

Read **Numbers 20:9-12**. What did Moses do instead?

_____

_____

_____

Moses did gather the people together, but instead of speaking to the rock, Moses hit it twice with his staff. How did God feel about this? What did He do?

_____

_____

God disapproved of what Moses did because he didn't obey His instructions completely. For this reason, God didn't allow Moses and Aaron to take the Israelites into The Promised Land.

Let's look at another example of someone who didn't obey completely. Read *1 Samuel 15:1-3*. What did God command King Saul to do in verse 3?

_____

_____

King Saul was told to kill all of the Amalekites and to destroy all that belonged to them. Read *1 Samuel 15:4-9*. What does Saul do?

_____

_____

It's easy to think that Saul obeyed God in this passage, but if we read carefully we can see that he didn't obey completely. He spared King Agag, who was king of the Amalekites, and also the best of the sheep and cattle. Read *1 Samuel 15:10-23*. What excuse does Saul give for his disobedience?

_____

_____

From the outside, it appeared like Saul had a valid reason to do what he did. He wanted to use the best of the sheep and cattle and sacrifice them to the Lord. He probably thought that slaughtering them was wasteful but using the animals in this way would glorify the Lord, so God would surely be ok with it right? Unfortunately for Saul, God did NOT agree with this reasoning. God tells Saul in verse 22 *"to obey is better than sacrifice"*. This message shows us the importance of obeying God's will. God says that obedience to Him is more important than any gifts, service, or sacrifices that we could offer Him. He wants a genuine relationship with us that's rooted in love and devotion. He doesn't want us to obey Him out of a sense of obligation or out of fear of being punished. He wants us to choose to obey Him because we love Him.

When God asks us to do something, He wants us to follow His instructions exactly. If we decide to do it our own way instead of God's way, it's rebellion. Take some time to pray. Ask God to reveal to you when you're not obeying Him all the way. Ask for help to show love and respect to Him and the adults He has placed in your life by obeying quickly and completely in the future.

COMPLETE WEEK 1 MEMORY VERSE WORK ON PAGE 62

SHOW TRUST, NOT DOUBT

Do your parents ever tell you to do things that seem confusing, like "Don't go over there" or "Don't go alone," and you're left wondering why? Even though the requests seem strange, it's still very important for you to obey your parents because they know what's best for you and are trying to keep you safe. Today let's read about two people from the Bible who also didn't have all the answers to some seemingly odd requests.

Read *Genesis 6:9-22*. What is God asking Noah to do?

_____

_____

_____

God asked Noah to do a strange job. He asked him to build a massive boat when there wasn't even a lake or an ocean around. This boat was 450 feet long, 75 feet wide, and 45 feet tall! The length alone was as long as 1 1/2 football fields! What do you think the people who were watching Noah build the ark were thinking?

_____

_____

_____

_____

Do you think it was easy for Noah to obey?   YES ◯   ◯ NO

Imagine if you were in Noah's position and God told you to build an ark because a huge flood was on its way. How would you feel about such an overwhelming responsibility? Could you find the faith to trust in God's plan, even if others doubted and opposed you?

_____

_____

_____

_____

Even though this seemed like a strange request, Noah didn't question God's instruction, the timing of it, or his ability to complete the task. What does it say that Noah did in verse 22?

_____

Let's look at another great example of a man who obeyed God when it was hard. Read **Genesis 12:1-9**. What does God ask of Abram in these verses?

_____

_____

Read **Hebrews 11:8**. Why was this hard for Abram to do? What did he not know?

_____

Abram followed God's instructions even though it was hard and he had no idea where he was going. Because he obeyed, God promised to bless Abram and give him a great nation of descendants, and He did.

Abram and Noah both obeyed because they had faith that God knew what He was doing and that He would give them understanding in time. Neither of them questioned God, asked for clarification, or required more information about what was going to happen next before they would obey. They both trusted God when it was very difficult.

Have you ever found yourself in a situation where your parents ask you to do something and you question whether you should really have to do it? Do you ever try to explain to them why you think their request isn't the best idea or try to justify your bad attitude towards it? Give an example of the last time that you did this and what their response was.

_____

_____

I hope that after today's lesson you can see why this behavior might be considered disobedient. When you feel like this, it's important to remember the significance of prayer. By seeking guidance from God, you can find the strength and wisdom to obediently prioritize God's will over your own desires and opinions. Wrap up today by praying and requesting God's help in following His will even when uncertainties arise.

COMPLETE WEEK 2 MEMORY VERSE WORK ON PAGE 63

OBEY WITH A JOYFUL ATTITUDE

In the past few days, we've discovered the many ways that God wants us to obey. Today, we're going to talk about one more important thing that God expects from us. To truly obey God we need to also obey with a joyful attitude.

Let's start by looking at **Deuteronomy 28**. In this chapter Moses describes to the children of Israel the blessings that will come with obedience and the curses that will come with disobedience. Read verses **47-48** and finish the verse.

"Because you did not serve the LORD your God

_____

in the time of prosperity, therefore in hunger and thirst, in nakedness and dire poverty, you will serve your enemies the LORD sends against you."

God gave the Israelites the land of Canaan as a gift. It was a land flowing with milk and honey, a promised inheritance that was meant to be cherished and appreciated. In return for this generous blessing, they should have responded with thankfulness, love, and joyful obedience, but sadly they often ignored God's instructions instead. They allowed their hearts to be swayed by worldly desires and let themselves be influenced by other nations. As a result of their disobedience, the Israelites found themselves in a state of servitude to their enemies.

When the Israelites failed to serve the Lord with joy, they were disobeying. God has given us life. He cares for us and blesses us. Our response should be one of gratefulness and a desire to serve and please the One who has done so much for us.

Read **Philippians 2:14** and copy the verse below.

_____

_____

This is a command, not a suggestion.

This means that we don't get to pick which things we will do with a joyful attitude and which we won't.

Read **Philippians 2:5-11**. How did Jesus obey God the Father? Did Jesus argue and whine as He obeyed or was His response full of love and willingness?

This lesson should have taught us 3 important reasons for joyful obedience:

1 WE SHOULD OBEY JOYFULLY OUT OF GRATITUDE FOR ALL GOD HAS DONE FOR US.

2 WE SHOULD OBEY JOYFULLY BECAUSE GOD HIMSELF COMMANDS IT.

3 WE SHOULD OBEY JOYFULLY BECAUSE OUR SAVIOR OBEYED HIS FATHER.

Write about a situation where you "technically" obeyed but were not joyful about it. Maybe you completed the task that was asked of you, but while you did it you were grumbling to yourself, stomping up the steps, rolling your eyes, or saying something rude or insulting to someone else. Do you think God or your parents see this as obedience or disobedience?

_____

_____

_____

Pray and ask God for help to reflect on the situation that you wrote about and see how you could have obeyed in a way that would have been pleasing to Him. Ask Him to help you obey with a joyful attitude in the future.

COMPLETE WEEK 2 MEMORY VERSE WORK ON PAGE 63

WHY DO I NEED TO OBEY?

So far we've learned that God really cares about obedience. He cares that we obey quickly, completely, and with a heart that is joyful and trusts Him. When we do this we not only please God but our obedience becomes an expression of our love for Him and a reflection of our devotion.

● ●

Have you been praying on your own for God's help in being obedient? Please write about any victories you've had this week. Have you had any failures? If so, did you ask for forgiveness?

_____

_____

_____

_____

As you get older and start to approach adulthood, you may question why it's important to listen to your parents. Let's explore what the Bible says for an answer!

Read **Colossians 3:20** and copy the verse below.

_____

_____

This verse gives the most obvious answer: Because God says to. It pleases God when you obey your parents. This also means when you disobey your parents God is not pleased. Look back at the verse. How does it say we should obey our parents?

_____

It says we should obey in everything or always. Parents have authority because God has given it to them. Obeying your parents might seem like a drain on your fun sometimes but obedience is for your own good because God knows what is best for you and your future.

Your parents see past the immediate "inconvenience" of finishing chores, saving money, or finishing homework to the ultimate good that these responsibilities bring.

Your parents have you do these things not to burden you but to train you. To succeed in life, you have to learn boundaries, be able to distinguish between right and wrong, and take on responsibilities. The rules and chores your mom and dad have in place are giving you a strong foundation to build on in the future when things get more challenging.

Read *Ephesians 6:1–3*. Copy verses 1-2 below.

_____

_____

_____

Paul quotes from the Ten Commandments here. It's good for children to obey their parents because it's what God commands. Obeying our parents is one way we show our parents and God that we love them.

Whether it's getting your chores done or just turning off the TV when you're told, obeying your parents is an important command given by God. It's much more than just doing what you're told; it's a reflection of your obedience to the Lord Himself and should model Christ's wholehearted obedience to the Father.

God purposely chose your parents to take care of you because He loves you and wants to keep you safe and happy. Give an example of some ways that your parents protect you by giving you rules, boundaries, and guidelines to follow.

_____

_____

_____

If these things don't always feel like God showing you His love it's only because we live in a broken world. Because of this brokenness, our earthly desire is to do things our own way. Pray and ask God to help you obey your parent's authority with a joyful attitude even when it feels difficult.

COMPLETE WEEK 2 MEMORY VERSE WORK ON PAGE 63

WHO DO I NEED TO OBEY?

Yesterday you learned about the importance of listening to your parents, but who else should you obey? The Bible tells us that as Christians we should also honor and obey those in authority over us.

God's intention for authority isn't about control or power games. It's about harmony and orderliness and He has a plan that's in motion through all of it, even when it doesn't make sense to us.

Read **Romans 13:1-2**. The governing authorities that exist were established by who?

_____

When we're under any form of leadership we are under God's authority. In your life these governing authorities might be:

Police Officers   **The Governor**   **The President**

To rebel against this authority is to rebel against who?

_____

This verse teaches us to obey governing authorities because they have been established by God himself.

In **John 19:8-11** what does Pilate say he has in verse 10?

_____

Pilate was the Roman governor of Judaea. Jesus is unwilling to answer Pilate's questions and Pilate makes sure Jesus understands that HE has the power to either free Jesus or condemn Him to crucifixion. How does Jesus respond?

"You would have no power over me...

_____ ."

Read *1 Peter 2:13–17*. Again, these verses tell us how God expects us to submit to the authorities He has placed over us. But what else is said in verse 16? Copy the verse.

_____

_____

God wants us to obey human authority, not because we're loyal to the government or people, but because we love and respect God and want to obey Him. As followers of God, we should never justify doing something bad just because the government says so. We must always remember that we answer to a higher power.

What happens when people in positions of power misuse their authority? Should we be blindly obedient to authority if that leader isn't following God?

Read *Acts 5:27-29*. What do Peter and the other apostles say in verse 29?

_____

While Peter and other apostles were commanded by Jewish authorities not to preach about Jesus, they chose instead to obey God rather than men. They recognized that human rules must never override God's rules.

The Bible does not support slave-like submission to leadership. Being under authority according to scripture means being willing to cooperate and obey leaders who are led by biblical wisdom and who use God's word to help them make their decisions. Before we end for the day, let's read about another group of people God wants us to obey.

Read *Hebrews 13:17*. This verse refers to your spiritual leaders. Spiritual leaders are mature Christians who speak the Word of God into your life and encourage your spiritual growth. We are called to joyfully submit to these leaders, so that their work will not be a burden, as long as they are following God and not altering His teachings. In your life these spiritual leaders might be your parents, grandparents, aunts and uncles, pastor, youth group leaders, or even older siblings.

Our obedience shows our trust in God's ultimate authority. Pray and ask God to help you obey the leaders in your life.

COMPLETE WEEK 2 MEMORY VERSE WORK ON PAGE 64

WHEN IT'S OK NOT TO OBEY

Let's start today by reviewing the key information that we learned over the last few days. Draw a line from the summary to the correct verse.

AUTHORITY IS GIVEN TO PEOPLE BY GOD

RESPECTING GOD'S ESTABLISHED AUTHORITY

AWARENESS OF THE DIFFERENCE BETWEEN HUMAN RULES & GOD'S RULES

WHO YOU SHOULD HAVE CONFIDENCE IN AND OBEY

HEBREWS 13:17

ROMANS 13:1-2

ACTS 5:29

JOHN 19:11

• •

Read *Daniel 3:1-30*. Why did Shadrach, Meshach, and Abednego refuse to obey the king?

_____

_____

Do you think it was easy for Shadrach, Meshach, and Abednego to obey God in this situation? Why or why not?

_____

_____

King Nebuchadnezzar ordered everyone to bow down to a golden statue. He even made a law saying that anyone who didn't bow would be thrown into a fiery furnace.

Shadrach, Meshach, and Abednego refused to bow down to the statue. They chose to obey God's rule regarding idols which says, "You shall not bow down to idols or worship them." Despite the risk of death, they remained faithful to God instead of obeying the king. How did God reward their obedience?

_____

_____

God rewarded their obedience by saving them from the fiery furnace. When the king saw how God had protected them, he told all of the people to honor and worship God.

Let's look at another story in the Bible about a man who followed God's rules instead of man's rules. In the book of Daniel, we learn that Daniel was a faithful man who always did what was right in God's eyes. He held a very important position as the king's most trusted official, which made the other officials very envious of him. They were so jealous that they devised a plan to remove Daniel from his position. They deceived King Darius into creating a law that would punish Daniel for praying to God. Read **Daniel 6:6-10**. What did Daniel do when he learned about the new law?

_____

_____

Daniel continued to pray to God, even when the new law was created. The men who were trying to catch him breaking this law were able to do so, and they persuaded the king to carry out his punishment, even though he didn't want to hurt Daniel. The king had to make a tough choice and commanded for Daniel to be placed in a den with lions for the night. The next morning, the king went to check on Daniel and discovered that he was unharmed, all thanks to God's protection. Read **Daniel 6:25-27**. What happened next?

_____

_____

_____

If you notice, the men in these stories only disobeyed when they were told to do something that went against what God wanted. It's important to respect our authority figures, even if they don't have the same beliefs as us. However, it's also important to know when we can politely disagree and stand up for what we believe is right. This doesn't mean we're being bad, but instead it shows that we listen to what God tells us. The stories of Shadrach, Meshach, Abednego, and Daniel teach us to stay true to our beliefs, even during very tough and scary times.

Pray and ask God to help you have a brave heart that follows His plans no matter what the circumstances.

COMPLETE WEEK 2 MEMORY VERSE WORK ON PAGE 64

THE LIMITS OF OBEDIENCE

Last week we discovered that it's ok to say no to a leader's instructions if they tell us to do something we know God wouldn't approve of. Today we're going to explore a few more scenarios where it's ok not to obey.

- **If an adult tells you to do something that is wrong or puts you or someone else in danger it's ok to say no and not obey.**

You know the difference between right and wrong and you have the right to protect yourself and others. Let's say a stranger comes to your house and wants to come inside while your parents aren't home. What should you do? Even though they are an adult and TECHNICALLY an authority, you should be very cautious in this situation. Opening the door to a stranger is risky because it could potentially put you in danger, so it's okay not to obey in this situation.

CAUTION CAUTION CAUTION CAUTION CAUTION CAUTION CAUTION CAUTION CAUTION CAUTION CAUTION CAUTION

- **When an authority goes too far and forgets the limits that God has set for them it's ok to say no and not obey.**

The Bible doesn't have a specific verse that states this exact message, but it has a lot of stories that support the idea that we don't have to obey when someone in charge tells us to do something that God hasn't given them permission to tell us. For instance, God doesn't give churches authority to create laws over people and He doesn't give governments the power to make decisions about who should or shouldn't be baptized.

Read **Mark 2:23-27**. In this example, Jesus tells the disciples they can pick and eat some grain from the field even though the Pharisees said it was forbidden on the Sabbath. Why? Copy verse 27 below.

_____

_____

It's not a sin to pick and eat some grain while walking through a field. The Pharisees may have said it was against the law, but since they didn't have the authority from God to make that decision the disciples didn't need to obey.

- **It's ok not to obey if someone does something or asks you to do something but then tells you NOT to tell your parents. If you have to hide something from your parents, it's best to say no and not obey.**

God commands us to obey our parents. If someone wants to do something but doesn't want your parents to know it's because they know your parents wouldn't approve. It's ok not to obey in this situation.

- **If you feel that an adult authority is trying to manipulate you, or they are doing things that make you feel uncomfortable, you should not obey.**

It's important to recognize that abuse can happen in any relationship, including those with adults who are supposed to be trustworthy and responsible. It can be difficult to speak up when you feel trapped or scared. If this happens find someone you trust like a family member, teacher, coach, or counselor. They can offer advice and help you come up with a solution.

Have you ever been in any of the 4 situations that were mentioned today? If so, what did you do?

_____

_____

_____

It's important to know that there ARE limits to obedience. God is in charge of everything and makes all the rules. You don't have to listen to anyone who tells you to do bad things, especially if it's against the law, dangerous, tricky, or goes against what you believe in. Always use God's Word to figure out which authority you should listen to and which ones you should stay away from because they are bad and can't be trusted.

Ask God for help in understanding which authorities you can trust. If someone makes you feel scared or uneasy, don't be afraid to say no. Talk to a responsible adult who can help keep you safe.

COMPLETE WEEK 3 MEMORY VERSE WORK ON PAGE 65

HEART TRANSFORMATION

So far in this study we've learned the ways that God expects us to obey. All of these are actions that you can physically see someone doing or not doing. But is it possible to obey on the outside and not on the inside?

Have you ever obeyed your parents when they were in the room but when they left the room you started doing what you had been asked to stop doing again?

YES ◯   ◯ NO

It's not enough for our outward actions to be pleasing if our hearts aren't in the right place. If you're motivated by wanting to merely please a person then you will only obey as long as they are keeping watch of your actions but not when they're no longer paying attention.

True Christian obedience requires a heart change - a transformation of our wills by God as we put our trust in Him - so that we strive to obey for His good pleasure. This internal transformation brings about an external transformation. It gives us a different mindset and a different source of motivation - we now WANT to do what's right rather than feeling like we're being forced to do what's right.

Read *Ephesians 6:5-8*. What is Paul saying here?

_____

_____

Paul is telling us that as Christians we need to serve from the heart with sincerity and good intentions, as if we were working for Christ directly and not for people.

Read *Hebrews 4:12-13*. What does it say that the Word of God does "*even to divide soul and spirit*"?

_____

God's Word penetrates us and exposes our true thoughts and attitudes. It's as if God goes in and performs heart surgery on us and because His Word is living and powerful, it speaks truth to the very core of who we are.

Copy **Hebrews 4:13** below.

_____

_____

Read **1 Samuel 16:7**. What does it say that God looks at?

_____

These verses tell us that nothing is hidden from God and He can see what's inside of us and in our hearts. He knows if we aren't obeying with the right attitude on the inside even if it looks like we are obeying on the outside.

Read **Jeremiah 17:10**. What does the Lord search and examine?

_____

Not only can God see what is in our hearts, but He also knows our thoughts.

Read **Romans 12:1-2** and finish the sentence below.

"Do not conform to the patterns of this world, _____
_____
."

To be conformed is to shape around something. This verse is telling us not to conform to the patterns of the world. We should strive to be conformed to the likeness and image of Jesus instead. We are then told that we should be transformed by the renewing of our minds. The renewing of our mind occurs when we are fully surrendered to God. When this happens, the Holy Spirit will breathe new life into us changing our hearts and minds to be obedient from the inside out.

True obedience from the heart happens from the inside out because it comes from the Spirit within us. Pray and ask God to breathe new life into you and to conform you to be more like Jesus. Ask Him to help you obey from the inside out.

COMPLETE WEEK 3 MEMORY VERSE WORK ON PAGE 65

CLEAN OUTSIDE, DIRTY INSIDE

Yesterday we learned that true obedience comes from the inside and it begins with God's work in our hearts. Let's look at an example from the Bible of some leaders who needed a heart transformation from God even though it seemed like they were obeying on the outside.

In the Old Testament, God gave the people of Israel the 10 commandments to help them live morally and make good choices. These rules were intended to shape not only their behaviors but also their inner thoughts and beliefs. However, over time, people started prioritizing outward obedience to these rules rather than genuinely obeying God from their hearts. Being able to see that someone obeyed became the only thing that seemed to matter. This shift led to a disconnect between people's actions and their true motives. The commandments, which were meant to guide them towards righteousness and moral living, became empty rituals that were followed without true understanding or conviction.

Read *Matthew 23:25-28*. Jesus has a lot to say to the teachers of the law and Pharisees about His disapproval of this behavior. What is He saying to them in these verses?

_____

_____

_____

Jesus warned them that although they may look clean on the outside, their hearts were dirty with greed, self-indulgence, hypocrisy, and wickedness within. They mistakenly thought that righteous acts performed in public, where others could see, justified them before God. Unfortunately, this had never been the case.

People's outward appearances can be misleading. Only you and God really know what's inside your heart and mind. Just like we take care of our physical health by keeping our bodies clean, it's equally important to focus on our spiritual and emotional well-being by praying, reflecting, and seeking guidance from God.

God holds us accountable for our negative thoughts and attitudes whether we act upon them or not. These inner struggles expose the true condition of our hearts. By acknowledging and addressing these thoughts and emotions, we can begin a journey of transformation and growth. God wants us to be honest with ourselves and with Him, admitting our weaknesses and asking for His guidance and forgiveness to overcome them.

Read **Psalms 139:23-24** and copy the verses below.

_____

_____

_____

David was a man after God's own heart, and although David despised those who spoke against God, he realized he wasn't perfect. He was very aware that sin might be lurking in his heart and mind. For this reason, David pleaded with the Lord to search his heart and know his thoughts. He asked that if God were to find any ungodliness in him that He would clean him up and lead him in a way that would please the Lord.

David understood that God looks at the heart. The outward appearance is what man values. God cares about our character and while we might be able to fool man, we never fool Him.

Obedience, whether on the inside or the outside, can be hard. It goes against our human nature because we live in a sinful and fallen world. The next time you're tempted to disobey, listen to the Holy Spirit inside of you and obey from your heart. The Spirit will empower you to do what's right in God's eyes. Don't live the life of a hypocrite. Be pure and clean both inside and outside.

Write out a prayer to God asking Him to change your heart and mind to mirror what His heart and mind are like. Ask God to show you where you're dirty on the inside and let Him clean you up.

_____

_____

_____

_____

COMPLETE WEEK 3 MEMORY VERSE WORK ON PAGE 65

JESUS, THE PERFECT TEACHER

As humans, we struggle with obedience because it calls us to humble ourselves rather than prioritize our wants and needs. Luckily, we have the perfect teacher and model of obedience in Jesus. Today we're going to learn how Jesus taught his disciples to be like Him. He did this through His example, explaining why character is important, highlighting other people's character, and correcting and encouraging others.

Jesus didn't just tell His disciples to follow Him, He explained the reasons WHY obedience is so important. Read *John 15:10* and copy it below.

_____

_____

_____

By following Jesus' teachings and commands, we demonstrate our trust in His wisdom and guidance. This obedience not only deepens our relationship with Him but also allows us to experience His love and blessings in our lives. As we align our actions with His will, we're able to witness the transformation and growth that comes from living a life centered on His teachings.

Jesus also taught the disciples HOW to obey and follow Him. Read *Matthew 16:24* and copy the verse below.

_____

_____

_____

Jesus teaches His disciples that the first step in obedience is to deny yourself. This means saying no to things that might feel good at the moment but will ultimately lead us away from God's path. It's through this difficult practice of denying our fleshly desires and instead choosing to follow God's will that we learn true obedience. This is a lifelong journey of aligning our hearts and minds with God's and trusting in His plans over our own.

27

Jesus gave correction and encouragement when it was needed. Read *Luke 10:38-42*. Why is Jesus telling Martha that what Mary has chosen is better?

_____

_____

Martha seems to be interested in Jesus' message. She invites Jesus to her home and He accepts. The problem is that her priorities aren't in the right place. She's more concerned about hosting Jesus than listening to Him. On the other hand, Mary submits entirely to Jesus and His message and that's why Jesus gives her encouragement.

In Martha's culture at the time, hospitality was considered one of the highest social expectations. In addition, in that culture, women were expected to serve, not to learn. Still, Mary sensed that Jesus was not just a regular teacher and wanted to know her true place in God's kingdom.

The Christian life is similar. Once the Holy Spirit makes His home in us, He will not leave. That doesn't instantly adjust our priorities into proper focus though. We can mirror Martha's well-meaning mistake by spending too much time on the basic outward expression of welcoming Jesus into our lives. That of course, can include some really good things like serving at church, listening to Christian radio, or hanging verses on our walls. But those things won't replace listening to His message and building a relationship with Him.

Read *1 John 2:3-6*. What is one way in which we naturally show that we have saving faith in Jesus?

_____

_____

We show God and others that our life belongs to Him through obeying His commands. This is true Christian obedience that delights in obeying because it is pleasing to the Lord.

Pray and ask God to help you to have character like Him. Ask God to help you prioritize what is most important like Mary and to humbly and joyfully obey His commands.

COMPLETE WEEK 3 MEMORY VERSE WORK ON PAGE 66

OBEDIENCE SHOWS YOUR TRUST

Abraham is acknowledged as one of the greatest models of obedience that exists in the Bible. On day 6, we learned that God called Abraham to leave his homeland and go to a land that God was still yet to show him. Abraham obeyed and left everything he knew behind and journeyed into the unknown. Despite the obstacles and uncertainties, Abraham obeyed without hesitation. Read **Genesis 22:2**. What does God ask him to do now?

_____

_____

_____

Abraham had originally trusted in God's promise that he would become the father of a great nation, even though he and his wife Sarah were very old and had no children. After a long 25-year wait God finally fulfilled His promise and gave them a son, who they named Isaac. Now Abraham's obedience is being further tested when God commands him to offer his only son Isaac as a sacrifice. Read **Genesis 22:3-14**. What happened next? Did Abraham obey?

_____

_____

_____

This test displayed the depth of Abraham's faith and his willingness to give everything he had to God, even his precious son that he had waited so long for. Abraham's obedience in this moment was incredible. He demonstrated unwavering trust in God, believing that even if he sacrificed Isaac God would still fulfill His promises. Abraham's obedience is a powerful example for us even today. It shows us the importance of trusting and obeying God, even when His commands may seem difficult. Because of his obedience, Abraham did not end up having to sacrifice Isaac and was greatly blessed.

Moses is another important biblical figure known for his complete trust in God, even in overwhelming circumstances. From being born and raised in Egypt to leading the Israelites out of slavery, Moses' life is full of inspiring moments of obedience.

One of the most well-known of these moments is when Moses leads the Israelites out of Egypt. Read *Exodus 14:1-14*. What is happening with Pharoah, the Egyptian Army, and the Israelites?

_____

_____

_____

_____

The Israelites unknowingly find themselves trapped between the Red Sea and the pursuing Egyptian Army. In this frightening and seemingly hopeless situation, Moses listens to God's instructions without question. Read *Exodus 14:15-31*. What happened next?

Moses is faced with what seems like an impossible task, yet he obeys and the Red Sea miraculously parts saving the Israelites and allowing them to cross to safety. End today by praying and asking God to give you trust in Him like Abraham and Moses displayed and an unwavering willingness to obey His divine instruction.

COMPLETE WEEK 3 MEMORY VERSE WORK ON PAGE 66

GIVE YOURSELF COMPLETELY

Today we're going to learn how obedience shows our love TO God and our love FOR God, as well as love to those around us. Jesus' life on earth was one ongoing expression of love for the heavenly Father through His unwavering obedience in the face of hardship. The night before His crucifixion, Jesus reminded the disciples of something very important. Read *John 14:21* and copy the verse below.

_____

_____

_____

_____

Jesus points out the connection between love and obedience and how they are inseparable. This means to love God is to obey Him and to obey God is to love Him.

Read *Philippians 2:8*. How did Jesus obey in this verse?

_____

Why did He do this? Read *Isaiah 53:5* and *John 3:16* and write your answer below.

_____

_____

_____

_____

Jesus obeyed the Father and willingly gave His life on the cross to atone for the sins of mankind. Because of this great display of love everyone is now offered an opportunity for salvation. This act not only shows Jesus' obedience to God but it is also the ultimate expression of God's love for humanity.

It's important to note that even though God <u>desires</u> obedience from us, God doesn't actually <u>need</u> anything from us. He didn't need to ask for help when He created the galaxies. He doesn't need our obedience, our work, or our money to make His desires become reality. He doesn't need us to worship Him or sing His praises in order to maintain His self-esteem.

So, when thinking about what we actually have to offer the Lord, the best thing we can give Him is <u>ourselves</u>. Completely surrendering in obedience to His will is one of the greatest gifts we can give to God and one of the best ways to show we love Him. Read **Romans 12:1**. What does God want from us?

_____

_____

Paul urges us to recognize that God has shown us an enormous amount of mercy. God owes us nothing. Instead of death, He has given us life and a purpose in Christ. He's forgiven our sins and shared Himself with us. We deserve absolutely none of that. So how should we respond?

Just as the Jewish people offered animals as sacrifices to God, Christians, in response to God's amazing gift of mercy, should instead offer <u>themselves</u> to Him as living sacrifices to be used for His purposes.

One way that we can be more like Jesus and offer ourselves to Him is by obeying the authority He has placed over us. Take a moment and list a few things that you can do to obey and show love to your parents (and God!) this week. <u>Make sure to do them</u>, remembering that these actions show our gratitude and love to God for all that He's done for us.

_____   _____

_____   _____

_____   _____

_____   _____

Pray and thank Jesus for His obedience on the cross and ask God to help you show love through your obedience this week.

COMPLETE WEEK 4 MEMORY VERSE WORK ON PAGE 67

OUR OBEDIENCE IS OUR WITNESS

As believers in Christ, we're all called to witness and share about God's greatness with those around us. But what does it mean to be a witness for Christ, why is it important, and how do we go about witnessing to others?

Read **Matthew 28:18-20**. What are we instructed to make? What are we instructed to teach them?

_____

_____

In these verses, which are also called The Great Commission, Jesus is giving us orders to witness and evangelize to others in order that more people would come to believe in His name and be saved. As Christians, we do this by giving a testimony to others about the truth of God that we have seen, experienced, and heard.

Can you think of the first time you heard the gospel? Who told you? How did they tell you? Did they first share Christ with you through their words or did you first notice Christ working in them through their actions?

_____

_____

_____

Sharing the gospel and being a witness doesn't always look like revival nights, youth group invitations, or mission trips. Sometimes, the most effective witness we can give is by showing our consistent everyday obedience to God.

It may be difficult to show up to church every Sunday morning when your friends are sleeping in or to obey God when it seems like those who aren't are having more fun. Walking in obedience to Christ isn't always flashy. But it's this normal, ordinary, everyday obedience that displays glory to God and shows His grace to the world.

Read *Isaiah 43:10-12*. What does God repeatedly say that you are in verses 10 and 12?

_____

Throughout all of scripture we can see God's people being called to be witnesses, which we do through our words and actions. Our lives should testify to the fact that we are God's children; we are set apart and redeemed and should live in a way that will show others WHO we belong to.

Read **1 Peter 2:9-10**. How does this make you feel?

_____

_____

You are God's special possession. You are chosen and set apart so that you can shout His praises. Wow, what an incredible blessing!

Your role as a witness is simply to share all that God has done in your life and what you know to be true about Him with others. God knows that when someone far from Him witnesses everyday consistent obedience in a Christian life it can have a powerful evangelistic effect. In this way, He can use your life and your submission to Him as a tool to draw others closer to Him.

On the flip side, disobedience or inconsistent obedience can be a poor witness, showing others that you don't take God seriously and that they probably shouldn't either.

Take a moment and think about the people in your life. Is there anyone that you wish was close to Christ that isn't? Write down the names of the people that God puts on your heart.

_____   _____   _____

Pray and thank God for His mercy and forgiveness and ask that He would use your life for His purposes. Pray and ask Him to draw the people that you wrote down close to Him. Ask God to help you to be a good witness to them through your words and actions.

COMPLETE WEEK 4 MEMORY VERSE WORK ON PAGE 67

THE BLESSINGS OF OBEDIENCE

Yesterday we learned that our obedience is a witness to others. When we obey God, our life shines a light that is so attractive to others that they can't help but see God. Today we're going to learn how obedience also brings blessings into our life.

Read **Luke 11:28** and copy the verse below.

_____

God's delight with human obedience is recorded repeatedly in Scripture. From faith filled leaders like Abraham, Noah, Moses, Joshua, and Daniel in the Old Testament to Mary, Jesus, Peter, and Paul in the New Testament, we see that God promises blessings for obedience and He always delivers.

Read **Psalms 1:1-6**. Can you explain what the author is trying to say in this Psalm?

_____

_____

Walking in the wisdom of God is the best way to live. This psalm tells us that those who obey God's teachings can avoid the consequences of sin and disobedience and in turn receive the blessing of a happy and fulfilled life. Think of God's Word as the instruction manual for our lives. When we apply its truths, our lives will function as God designed them to.

Picture a man who buys an unassembled swing set for his kids. He has no experience building things or working with tools, but if he reads the manual and follows the instructions he'll be able to put it together correctly. Then he and his children will be rewarded. If he ignores the owner's manual and decides that he can "just tell" how everything is supposed to fit together, he's probably in for a disaster. Plainly put, there are built-in rewards for simply following the instructions.

Let's look at an example of when Peter says yes to God. Read *Luke 5:1-11*. Was Peter blessed by his obedience?

YES ◯   ◯ NO

Yes, in fact a lot of people were blessed by Peter's obedience. The noisy crowd received the first blessing because they could now clearly hear Jesus' words. Jesus also benefited by being able to sit down in comfort as He preached.

When Jesus finished with His lesson, He gave Peter another opportunity to say yes or no. Look back at verse 4, what does Jesus say?

_____

Peter probably felt tempted to say no. He had just been out fishing the entire night and had returned with nothing to show for it. Now this young teacher was asking him to go fishing again? In the end, Peter ends up choosing to obey Jesus. In *Luke 5:5-11* what happened as a result of Peter's obedience?

_____

_____

Saying yes to Jesus' request resulted in a miracle that transformed not only Peter's life but also the lives of the entire group of fishermen. This is a great example of how obeying God in the small, seemingly insignificant things is an important step in receiving God's blessings. It also is an example of how God often blesses others—in particular, those closest to us—as a result of our obedience. We can see this when a parent obeys God and the entire family is rewarded with God's blessings, or when a child's obedience blesses his or her parents.

What blessings have you experienced in your life as a result of following God's commands?

_____

_____

Take a moment to thank God for each blessing that you listed above.

COMPLETE WEEK 4 MEMORY VERSE WORK ON PAGE 67

WHY IS OBEDIENCE IMPORTANT?

Today we'll take some time to review what we've learned so far. Our obedience to God demonstrates our trust and faithfulness in Him, proves our love for Him, glorifies Him in the world through our witness, and creates a way for God to bless us.

Our faith is essential in order to please God, and if the faith we have in our hearts is sincere, we will live a life that strives to be more like Christ each day. We'll obey His commands, not because we have to, but because we want to out of love and gratitude. We become empowered to obey after we believe because the Holy Spirit comes to live within us and we're changed from the inside, being remade into a new person.

Read *2 Corinthians 5:17* and copy the verse below.

_____

_____

When we obey God we can live a life filled with joy and peace that surpasses any earthly understanding. that is deeply rooted in the Lord and fully confident in our hope of heaven.

Because we live in a corrupt world that opposes God's values, our Christian character traits stand out and show that we walk in the light in an otherwise dark world.

Read *John 3:19-20*. Why does everyone who does evil hate the light and refuse to come into it?

_____

Light can brighten even the darkest parts of our hearts and minds, making us face our deepest fears and insecurities. Some people hesitate to welcome Jesus into their lives because His teachings and actions push us to confront our flaws and make changes in our lives.

Read **John 3:21**. This verse says that *"whoever lives by the truth comes into the light"* so that what will happen?

_____

_____

By obeying God and displaying His love and character to those around us, we not only glorify Him but also show that He is actively working in the world.

Read **Psalms 128:1** and copy the verse below.

_____

_____

Fear of the Lord stems from knowing Him and understanding His greatness, power, and holiness. Our God is the eternal God who spoke the universe into existence. This great and powerful Creator is also absolutely holy and we have violated His holy standards. Through Jesus, He invites us to draw near to Him, but we must always do so with reverence and awe. The fear of the Lord results in obedience to Him and will naturally cause us to "walk in His ways."

Read **Proverbs 8:13. "The fear of the Lord is to hate _____ ."**

Read **2 Corinthians 7:1**. Why are we purifying ourselves?

_____

We want to make ourselves clean in body and spirit by removing anything that goes against God in our daily lives. We do this out of fear, respect, and love for Him. If we are truly growing in the knowledge of God, we should also be growing in the fear of God. When we're tempted to sin, even if no one else is watching, we will remember that God is always watching.

We can either do life God's way or our way. I hope this study is helping you to understand why obedience is so important and why we need to obey God's instructions and do things His way. Hopefully you have been finding it easier to obey each day with the help of the Holy Spirit guiding you. End today by praying. Ask God to help you obey with gladness and trust and to give you the wisdom and courage to live a life that is pleasing to our awe inspiring heavenly Father.

COMPLETE WEEK 4 MEMORY VERSE WORK ON PAGE 68

DON'T LET PRIDE GET IN THE WAY

The longer I am a Christian, the more I'm realizing that God's commands — like the command to be humble — aren't hard to find. They're hard to obey.

When we're prideful, we think more highly of ourselves than we should. This is a position that goes directly against who Jesus calls us to be. Jesus calls all who follow Him to carry their crosses, which includes putting to death our exaggerated, false sense of self-importance.

Let's look at an example from the Bible. Read **Genesis 11:1-9**. What were the people trying to do?

_____

_____

Why did God think this was a problem?

_____

The mistake wasn't the tower itself, but the belief that they could reach God by building it. It was a big mistake to think they could reach Heaven through their own actions. Only God's grace can lead us to Heaven. To make things worse, they said, "let us make a name for ourselves." Not only were they trying to enter Heaven on their own, but they were also seeking fame. That's pride with a capital P!

Now let's take a look at a great king from the Bible. Read **2 Chronicles 1:1**. Solomon had more riches than any other king and had just been put in charge of one of the most powerful nations on earth. Do you think it would be easy to get just a little bit proud?

YES ◯   ◯ NO

Read **2 Chronicles 1:7-10**. What does Solomon ask God for?

_____

God appeared to Solomon in a dream and asked Solomon if there was anything he wanted. Despite his earthly greatness, Solomon was humble enough to ask for wisdom from God to govern God's people. Read *2 Chronicles 1:11-12*. What was God's response?

_____

_____

Solomon became very rich and wise. He used some of his wealth to build a temple for God. Read *2 Chronicles 6:13*. After the temple was built, what did Solomon do to dedicate the temple?

_____

Solomon prayed and acknowledged God's greatness in front of all of Israel.

Solomon showed humility by kneeling down and showing that he needed God's help and was willing to listen to God's commands. Read *2 Chronicles 6:14-21*. Was Solomon's prayer a proud prayer or a humble prayer? How can we tell?

_____

_____

Humility is acknowledging our own weakness and admitting that we need help from God, just like Solomon did. Humility and obedience go hand in hand; without one, the other is nearly impossible. Pride is the enemy of obedience because it causes us to prioritize ourselves rather than God and others. When we're prideful we refuse to admit our sinfulness and we demand to do things on our own, without help from God or anyone else.

What are some things that you are tempted to be prideful about? Are there things in your life that you are not willing to ask for help for?

_____

_____

Pray and ask God to help you to overcome the pride in your life. Ask that He would humble you and allow you to put His desires before your own.

COMPLETE WEEK 4 MEMORY VERSE WORK ON PAGE 68

YOU'RE GOING TO FAIL AND THAT'S OK

During your time at church, you may have learned how Jesus is perfect because He is the Son of God. Unfortunately, it's not possible for humans to be perfect in this corrupt world. Instead, God calls us to be continually growing to be more like Jesus.

Take a moment right now and flip back to Day 12 where we talked about heart transformation and read the underlined sentence in the 4th paragraph from the top. Fill in the following blank.

Our heart transformation, or internal transformation, brings about _____.

This progression of being transformed and becoming more like Christ over time is called sanctification. This is a really big word that simply means "to make holy or to set apart" for the sole purpose of serving or honoring God. When God sanctifies us, He sets us apart from the rest of the world.

I'm going to throw another big word at you now- justification. Justification is an act of God through grace, where He declares a sinner to be righteous because of their faith in Jesus. We are justified at the moment of our salvation. This is a one-time event where God

Hello, I AM
MADE RIGHT BEFORE GOD, SAVED, BLAMELESS, REDEEMED, SET FREE

removes your "sinful" label and it's thrown away forever. Disobedient actions can't take this new identity from you.

On the other hand, sanctification is not a one-time event. This is something that takes place over the rest of our Christian lives. Even though God washes us clean and our

Hello, I AM
A WORK IN PROGRESS, FOLLOWING THE HOLY SPIRIT TO BE MORE LIKE CHRIST

sins won't be held against us on the day of judgment, this doesn't mean that all of a sudden we'll be completely free from sins power in our life. Sin is still active and present in the world, and we will still sometimes listen to it and make the wrong choices.

41

There are going to be times that we will fail and it's important to recognize that when we fail that failure doesn't become our identity - our identity still remains in Christ. Read *Romans 8:28* and copy the verse below.

_____

_____

Failures can't rob us of our God-given identity and purpose. On the contrary, God can use our failures to actually move us closer to that purpose.

Read *Philippians 3:12-14*. What goal do you think Paul is referring to?

_____

Knowing that he could never be perfect in his earthly life, Paul's one goal is to pursue becoming more like Christ. He is teaching us that failures are not final. We can learn from the past, but we aren't controlled by the things we've done. As new creations in Christ, each day you are blessed with a whole new chance to be honest, own up to mistakes, take responsibility, walk with integrity, apologize, and try to make a better decision the next time. This means that each day is also an opportunity to make less excuses, stop being so defensive, and stop trying to act like you don't make mistakes.

Read *Psalms 37:24* and copy the verse below.

_____

_____

It pleases God to see us learning and growing from each other when we stumble. He is our stronghold and through Him we can get more out of our mess-ups than what we lost. In this way, let your failures plant seeds for blessings rather than feed fears and anxiety.

Pray and thank God for giving you a special identity; one that is better than anything you could ever earn through your own effort. God loves you and thinks you're amazing, mistakes and all!

COMPLETE WEEK 5 MEMORY VERSE WORK ON PAGE 69

ACTIONS SPEAK LOUDER THAN WORDS

Your actions speak. The question is what are they saying? In regards to our faith, if our words and actions are saying different things we have to look at our actions for the truth of what is really in our hearts. Read **James 2:18**. What is James saying?

_____

_____

James is saying that a true saving faith in Jesus results in bringing about good works in us. This is a result of the heart transformation that we have already discussed. What does it show when a person who claims to have faith doesn't produce any good works in their life?

_____

This is a false faith. How we react and the actions we take are the direct result of what we truly believe. Simply claiming to have faith in Christ is meaningless; saving faith is a faith that results in action. Read **1 John 3:18** and copy it below.

_____

_____

Read **Matthew 7:16-20**. What are these verses telling us?

_____

_____

People might seem super religious, but over time, you'll see their true character. Do their actions align with their words? Do they stay faithful to God when no one's around?

Next, we're going to read about a time when Jesus was teaching in the temple and was confronted by chief priests and elders who tried to trip Him up with a question. Jesus responds by telling them a parable with some questions of its own. This forces these religious leaders to confront and attempt to hide the real motives of their hearts.

Read *Matthew 21:28-32*. Which son did what his father wanted? Give a reason for your answer.

_____

_____

Just to be clear, both sons were disobedient. <u>Delayed obedience is still disobedience</u>; a great reminder to obey right away! The Parable of the Two Sons is told by Jesus to teach the importance of obedience and repentance. In the parable, a father asks his two sons to go and work in his vineyard. The first son initially refuses, but later has a change of heart and goes to work. The second son happily agrees but never bothers to do it. Jesus wants us to realize that what we do is more important than what we say we'll do. Again, actions speak louder than words. We don't want to claim to be someone that we're not.

This parable tests us to examine our own hearts and actions. Are you making obedience in your relationship with God a priority? This includes actively obeying your parents and leaders quickly, completely, without questioning or doubting them, and with a joyful heart.

YES ⬤   ⬤ NO

Is there any conflict between your outward expression of faith and your actions? If so, list where it's conflicting in your life below.

_____

_____

_____

List specific action steps that you will take to combat and eliminate these conflicts.

_____

_____

_____

Our actions reveal where our faith really is. Pray and ask God to help you with any conflicts that you listed above. Ask for guidance to follow His will so that your life can be full of good fruit and works in His name.

COMPLETE WEEK 5 MEMORY VERSE WORK ON PAGE 69

CONSEQUENCES OF DISOBEDIENCE

Today we're going to look at the flip side of obedience. What are some of the outcomes we experience in life when we don't take obedience seriously?

⭐ Disobedience distances us from God

The Bible warns that disobeying God makes us feel distant from Him. It's like when you know you should listen to your parents, but you choose to ignore their advice. Sometimes, when we don't do what we should, we might feel separated from God because we know deep down that we haven't been acting in a way that pleases Him. It's like a little cloud that comes between us and God, making us feel distant.

Read *Isaiah 59:2* and copy the verse below.

_____

_____

This distant feeling is kind of like when you do something wrong, and you feel like you can't talk to your friend until you say sorry. In the same way, when we sin it creates a barrier between us and God.

Thankfully, God is always ready to forgive us and welcome us back with open arms when we apologize and change our ways. So even if you feel distant, you can always find your way back to Him with a humble heart and a desire to do better.

Write about a time when you didn't obey. When you think about how it made God feel, does it make you feel closer or farther away from Him?

_____

_____

_____

⭐ Disobedience causes missed blessings

Ignoring God's guidance and doing things our own way may prevent us from experiencing the blessings and opportunities He has in store for us. The Bible has many stories that teach us this important lesson.

One of these stories is about Adam and Eve who were given a perfect paradise called the Garden of Eden. Sadly, they made a big mistake. They didn't listen to God and ate from the forbidden tree. As a result, they were forced to leave their beautiful home and were no longer able to be close to God. It was a heartbreaking consequence for their actions.

Another example is Saul, who was the first king of Israel. Even though God chose him to lead His people, Saul let his pride and impatience get the best of him. He didn't follow God's specific instructions and did things his own way. As a result, he lost his kingdom and God's favor.

Write about a time when you didn't follow the rules or didn't listen to your mom and dad. What happened as a result? Did you miss out on something good because of it?

_____

_____

_____

Sometimes, when we mess up it can be tough to look beyond the consequence that we get and see the blessings we could have had. For example, if we get in trouble and get grounded we might miss the blessing of enjoying our freedom. Or if we tell a lie we risk losing the trust of our parents, which is a valuable blessing. It's important to remember that our actions have consequences and can affect the good things in our lives.

End today by praying and asking God to help you obey and stay on the path that is pleasing to Him. Seek His help to give you the strength to carry out His will, so you can experience the amazing blessings He has in store for you.

COMPLETE WEEK 5 MEMORY VERSE WORK ON PAGE 69

MORE CONSEQUENCES OF DISOBEDIENCE

Yesterday we learned that when we don't obey God and we decide to do things our own way He might feel distant, and we might miss out on the good blessings He has planned for us. Today we will learn a few more consequences of disobedience.

⭐ Disobedience gives Satan an opportunity

Satan is delighted when he notices that God's children aren't obeying His rules. He waits for opportunities when believers aren't focused on God, and then he swoops in to cause mischief. His goal is to make us desire things, become easily distracted, and question God, all in order to lead us astray. Satan knows that by separating us from God he can gain a strong hold in our lives and create chaos and suffering. He enjoys the mess he creates and finds joy in the pain and trouble he causes.

Read *Ephesians 4:26-27* and copy these verses below.

_____

_____

_____

This verse is specifically about disobedience due to anger. When someone gets really mad it can be like giving the devil an invitation to cause problems. Instead of reasoning things out people may react impulsively, letting their emotions control their actions instead.

Holding onto anger and keeping it bottled up, even if it's for a good reason, can turn into bitterness over time. The longer we hold onto anger, the more opportunities the devil has to spread negativity and hate. That's why we're told not to go to bed angry, so the devil can't twist things around and deceive us with his lies.

When faced with challenges, as believers we should stay strong in our faith, believing in God's wisdom and grace to overcome the challenges Satan throws our way.

⭐ Disobedience leads to no fruitfulness.

Read **John 15:5**. Without God how much good fruit can you produce?

_____

You can't grow ANY good fruit if you keep disobeying God. Trying to be fruitful without Him is like trying to swim against a strong current - exhausting and pointless. We need to be obedient to God and follow His guidance in order to bear the fruits of a fulfilling and purposeful life.

⭐ Disobedience invites God's discipline.

Read **Hebrews 12:5-6**. What's the _"word of encouragement that addresses you as a father addresses his son?"_

_____

_____

_____

_____

Just like a loving parent disciplines their child, God also corrects and guides us because He cares about us. So when He disciplines us, we shouldn't "lose heart" by feeling sad or discouraged. We should view it as an opportunity to grow spiritually and become more mature.

God's discipline can show up in many different ways. He might use problems at school or home, at church, or even with our friends. Sometimes, He might let us face difficult times, sickness, or even losing someone we love.

Read **Proverbs 13:24**. The one who loves their children does what?

_____

The Bible tells us that discipline is an act of love. It's not about being mean but is about teaching what is right.

Pray and thank God for His loving discipline. Ask Him to guide you in making good choices that produce good fruit and don't give Satan any opportunities.

COMPLETE WEEK 5 MEMORY VERSE WORK ON PAGE 70

RELATIONSHIP PROBLEMS

So far we've learned that disobeying God has some pretty big consequences! It creates distance between us and God, causes us to miss out on blessings that He wants for us, gives Satan a chance to create chaos in our lives, leads us to produce no good fruit, and also gives God a reason to discipline us. Whew! If you thought that was bad, today we'll discuss another way that disobedience can cause problems in our lives.

⭐ Disobedience creates problems in our relationships

The Bible emphasizes the importance of listening to God. When we don't listen to Him it can cause problems in our relationships with our family members and with the people in our community.

Read *1 Corinthians 3:1-3*. Why is Paul calling them "*worldly*" and "*mere infants in Christ*"?

He wants them to understand that they still have a lot to learn about God's love and teachings. They are acting like spiritual babies who need to discover what it truly means to follow Jesus. Even though they have the Holy Spirit, they're still too focused on themselves, arguing and feeling envious of one another. Because of this, instead of getting closer to God they are stuck in their selfish ways.

By pointing out these things, Paul hopes they will think about their behavior and concentrate more on growing spiritually. Their disobedient actions are getting in the way of their relationship with God and are stopping them from fully embracing His love and teachings.

God's wisdom and guidance help us to have healthy and happy relationships with others. God wants us to follow His commandments, which teach us to love, respect, and understand each other. If we don't listen to God, we might have conflicts and misunderstandings within our family or in our community.

When we ignore God's guidance we might do things that hurt others, like lying or cheating. This can make our relationships with others hard and cause a lot of pain.

Write about a time when you ignored God's guidance and ended up hurting someone's feelings. Which one of God's commands did you ignore that could have prevented this from happening?

_____

_____

_____

_____

Write about a time when you were fighting with a family member or friend. What happened? Did the problem get fixed? How did it affect your relationship with this person?

_____

_____

_____

_____

Write about a time when you told a lie and got caught. When the other person found out that you lied how did it make them feel? How did their reaction make you feel? Was it worth it?

_____

_____

_____

_____

Disobeying God's rules can have a huge impact on our relationships. It can make others feel upset or angry with us. It can also make people not trust us as much or want to spend time with us anymore.

Pray and ask God to help you follow His rules so that you can be kind and respectful to everyone around you. Pray for good relationships with others so you can show them Jesus' love by doing what God wants.

COMPLETE WEEK 5 MEMORY VERSE WORK ON PAGE 70

DISOBEDIENCE HURTS OUR WITNESS

Last week we discovered that when we don't follow what God has taught us it can make our relationships suffer. Lying, cheating, gossiping, jealousy, and other unhealthy behaviors show that we don't care about others, and it can cause problems like fighting, broken trust, and hurt feelings. This is connected to what we'll learn today too.

On Day 17, we learned that when we listen and obey it can be a witness of our faith to those around us. But what about when we don't obey? Sadly, it has the opposite effect and can send a negative message instead.

⭐ Disobedience hurts our Christian witness

Read *1 Corinthians 6:19-20*. What do these verses tell us?

_____

_____

Your life is not your own. As a believer, God paid a high price for you and now you bear His name. Because of this, you're called to honor God with your body by living in a way that shows others His love and kindness. When you live in a way that makes God happy, you're expressing your gratitude for all that He has done for you.

Read *Titus 2:6-8*. Why is it important to act our best, especially when non-believers are watching us?

_____

_____

_____

When we misbehave in front of people who don't believe, they might think negatively about us AND God. This can make people think less of us and our faith. It can confuse people when we act in a way that goes against what we say we believe. They might not understand why we say one thing but do another. This can make them question if we really believe what we say we do.

Also, when people see us misbehaving they might think that our behavior represents what our faith is all about. This can make them think negatively about God and not take our beliefs seriously. If they see us as examples of our faith, our actions can either make them interested in God or push them away.

The consequences of misbehaving in front of non-believers extend beyond just their opinions of us. It can also impact their perception of God and their willingness to explore a relationship with Him. If they see us as representatives of our faith, our actions can either attract or repel them from considering a relationship with God.

Not doing what God says can happen in many ways, like being dishonest, holding onto anger or not forgiving, giving in to things we know are wrong, or not doing what we're supposed to do. These things go against what Jesus taught us and what Christianity stands for. When people see us acting in this way it can make them think that Christianity is fake or not important, and they might even decide to stay away from it.

Look back to yesterday's lesson on page 50. Do you think being disobedient in the situations you wrote about made it harder for you to show the people you were in conflict with what it means to be a good Christian? YES ◯ ◯ NO

Do you think that in any of those situations the other person saw your actions and also saw a glimpse of the good things that happen when we give our lives to Jesus?

YES ◯ ◯ NO

When we're honest, kind, and caring we can share God's love with others. By acting this way we're not only showing gratitude to God, but we're also demonstrating how wonderful He is to those who may not know Him yet. Our actions and words have power and can influence others and bring them closer to God's love and truth.

When we choose to go against what God tells us to do it never leads to anything good. Pray and thank God for forgiving you when you make mistakes and ask Him to guide you in being a good example to others by doing what He wants you to do.

COMPLETE WEEK 6 MEMORY VERSE WORK ON PAGE 71

GOD GIVES US HIS WORD

Today we're going to learn about an amazing tool from God that can help us when we're doing our best to follow His commands. Read **Psalms 119:11** to discover this tool. What can we do that will help keep us from sinning?

_____

_____

It goes without saying that obedience to God's Word is impossible if you don't know what it says. Hiding God's Word in our hearts, or memorizing scripture, helps us to be more obedient and grow in our faith. By intentionally memorizing God's Word we allow it to guide our thoughts, attitudes, and actions. Read **Psalms 119:105** and copy the verse below.

_____

_____

Memorizing scripture helps us to obey because it fills our hearts and minds with God's Word. When we know what God wants us to do, it's easier to follow His instructions and make good choices. The more we remember, the more we can rely on it to guide us in our daily lives. Scripture helps us to remember what is right and encourages us to live in a way that pleases God.

When we learn and remember God's Word it brings peace to our hearts, stops us from doing sinful things, and shows us the right way to live our lives. If those truths weren't enough, there are even more amazing reasons to make this a part of our everyday life...

⭐ Jesus memorized scripture

To be more like Jesus, we are encouraged to follow His example. Throughout the Bible, there are many stories about Jesus using scripture. One of the most well-known times is when Jesus was in the desert and Satan tried to trick him.

Read **Matthew 4:1-11.** How many times does Jesus quote scripture to combat what Satan is tempting Him with?

_____

⭐ It brings us closer to God

Reading God's Word makes our faith stronger, helps us connect with God, and gives us guidance when things are tough. It brings us closer to God when we pray and reflect on what He's teaching us. When we focus on the promises and truths in the Bible, we can find peace and grow spiritually by better understanding what God wants for us.

⭐ We better understand right and wrong

The Bible is like a special guide that helps us know what's good and bad in the world. It tells us that we should love God with all our heart, mind, soul, and strength, and also love others just like we love ourselves. God wants us to study and follow His instructions for how to live our lives so that we can live our best lives through His direction.

⭐ We can support our Christian friends

Read **1 Thessalonians 4:18** and copy the verse below.

_____

The scriptures are meant to motivate and encourage us as we journey through life. If we remember God's Words we can pass them on to our friends, who also believe, as a way to give them comfort and make them stronger in their faith when they need them.

There are so many good things that happen when we study scripture! Take some time and write out a prayer to God. Tell Him that you want to understand His Word better and use what He teaches you in a meaningful way. Ask Him to reveal new things to you as you place scripture in your heart so that you can grow closer to Him.

_____

_____

_____

_____

COMPLETE WEEK 6 MEMORY VERSE WORK ON PAGE 71

GOD GIVES US PRAYER

Yesterday we learned about memorizing God's Word and how God gives this tool to us to help us obey. Let's take a look at another tool that God gives us - prayer. Read *Isaiah 65:24*. When we pray how will God respond?

_____

_____

When we pray to God He hears us and answers!

The next time you're finding it hard to obey remember this verse and take a moment to pray for help. But how can we be sure He will say yes? Let's find out.

Prayer is a powerful tool. It's our way of talking to God and it shows that we know that He is in control. When we pray, we let go of our own wishes and desires and focus on His.

Jesus is the perfect example of prayer in the garden of Gethsemane. Read *Luke 22:42*. Jesus didn't want to suffer on the cross. Yet in the same breath He prayed to the Father saying what? Copy verse 42 below.

_____

_____

Jesus was fully committed to obeying His Father's will. Read *John 4:31-34*. What does Jesus say that His food is?

_____

_____

Jesus came to earth with a very important mission: to always do what His Father wanted. He taught us how to listen and obey the Father's will. For believers, "Not my will, but yours be done" is the prayer that never fails. Read *1 John 5:14* and copy the verse below.

_____

_____

_____

John talks about how important it is to have confidence when praying. If you pray in a way that matches God's Word and what He wants, you can trust that He will hear you and respond. But God doesn't just give us anything we ask for like a vending machine. He listens to us, but He answers our prayers according to His own plans.

Read **James 4:3** and write or draw what you believe it means below.

When we pray, we should have the right motivation. Selfish motives will not be blessed by God.

Do you think praying and asking God to help you be obedient matches His Word and what He wants?

YES ⭘   ⭘ NO

Prayer is a special tool that God gives us to help us obey. When we pray to be obedient we ask God to show us the right way and make our hearts want what He wants. What other ways does prayer help us be obedient?

- Prayer gives us the power to resist doing bad things and to choose what's good.
- Praying for obedience strengthens our trust in God.
- When we pray, we feel even closer to God and more connected to Him.

Obedience is more than just following rules. It comes from deep love and gratitude and acknowledging that God's wisdom surpasses our own. Because of this, we choose to follow His lead and let Him guide us. Pray and ask God with all of your heart to guide you in believing and following Him wholeheartedly.

COMPLETE WEEK 6 MEMORY VERSE WORK ON PAGE 71

56

GOD'S TOOL: SUFFERING

Have you ever thought about why Jesus had to go through so much suffering when He came to earth as a human? You might think that since He is the Son of God He should have had a nice and easy life and a quick and painless death. Read **Hebrews 5:8**. What did Jesus learn through His suffering?

_____

Jesus chose to feel what it's like to be weak and suffer like humans do, but He also chose to experience learning and growth through these struggles.

Read **2 Corinthians 1:8-11** and copy the second sentence of verse 9 below.

_____

_____

_____

Paul talks about a really tough situation he and his friends went through in Asia. They were under so much pressure and felt like they couldn't handle it anymore. It was really hard for them, and they started to lose hope in life. Paul says that God used these tough times to show them that they should rely on Him, not themselves. It wasn't just random suffering; it was a way for God to teach them and help them grow stronger in their faith. So even though the suffering was uncomfortable and challenging, it was good, because it brought about a heart transformation in them.

If you've been a Christian for a while you know that you should trust God. You know that you were made to have a close relationship with Him, and you realize that life goes much smoother when you follow His teachings. However, the reality is...we don't always live up to it. That is, until something unfortunate happens and we end up on the floor (sometimes literally) pleading to God saying, "I can't handle this!" And it's in that desperate and painful place that we go from just knowing we should trust God to actually trusting Him.

Whether it's the little problems we face every day or a big change in our lives, God uses our pain and suffering to make our hearts better in a way that nothing else can. Our God is good, gracious, and in control of everything. The suffering we go through is not random or pointless; it's part of God's plan for us. We can trust that when God allows us to suffer, it's for our own good.

Read **Romans 5:3-5** and list the things that suffering produces:

P_____   C_____   H_____

When we face difficulties it's easy to feel like we're drowning in them. But, like the Apostle Paul said, these tough times can actually help us grow and change for the better. Just like a diamond is made under pressure, our character can become stronger and more refined through tough situations. When we push through hard times we build up our strength and endurance. We learn to lean on our inner power and beliefs to get past obstacles. This strength not only helps us deal with current challenges but also gets us ready for any future struggles that might come our way.

Going through tough times shapes who we are and how we see the world. It can teach us to be humble, empathetic, and thankful. We start to feel more for others who are going through hard times, and we learn to be more grateful for the good things in our lives.
Most importantly, facing hard times can give us hope. As we conquer obstacles and come out stronger on the other side, we start to believe in our ability to handle anything that comes our way. We understand that tough times won't last forever and that we have the strength and resilience to get through any storm.

In the end, finding joy in tough times isn't about ignoring the challenges we're facing, but about seeing them as chances to grow and change. By facing adversity with bravery and faith we can come out stronger, kinder, and full of hope for what's to come.

Pray and thank God for His ability to ultimately turn bad moments in our lives into something good. Ask Him to continue to help you learn and grow through your struggles.

COMPLETE WEEK 6 MEMORY VERSE WORK ON PAGE 72

OBSTACLES TO OBEDIENCE

Obeying what God says may seem like such an easy thing, but it's not always that simple. Sometimes it can be really hard to do what God asks of us. We're going to finish this study by learning about things that can get in the way of our obedience so that through God's strength we can recognize and overcome them when they are in our lives.

Fear

Being afraid is like a big wall in our way! It could be fear of rejection or being made fun of. Or maybe we're afraid of taking risks and failing. Fear is Satan's trick to stop us from doing what God wants. He knows that if we let fear control us, we'll never find the courage to follow God's guidance.

Read *Joshua 1:9* and copy the verse below.

_____

_____

_____

_____

Hold on tight to God and be brave enough to confront your fears head-on. This requires courage and determination, and it means stepping out of your comfort zone. This powerful combination is an act of surrender and trust, and it empowers us to overcome obstacles, defeat the Devil, and follow God's commands with obedience. By embracing this mindset, we can live a life filled with faith, courage, and unwavering devotion to our Creator.

Pride

Do you ever not do what you're told because you're worried that people won't like you or will think less of you? Or do you believe that you've achieved so much on your own that you're too important to listen to God? That's called being prideful.

Read **Psalm 10:4**. Copy the verse below.

_____

_____ʲ_____

_____

Some people believe they can handle everything on their own without God's guidance. These people often choose to disregard God and His teachings. They prioritize their own desires and overlook what's right and wrong in God's eyes. Their minds and hearts are closed to God as they are consumed by their selfish behavior.

Unbelief

Sometimes it's difficult to believe that God can work through us to accomplish His plans. We might question ourselves and have doubts, thinking that because we're not a "perfect" Christian or a Bible expert God wouldn't be able to use us.

Read **Mark 9:23** and copy below what Jesus says.

_____

God is powerful and can do anything He promises. He can use you just the way you are. All you have to do is listen to Him, trust Him, and have faith.

Busyness

Being too busy can stop us from doing what God wants us to do. We get caught up in our own to-do lists and can get distracted from what's really important.

Read **Ephesians 5:15-17**. How should we live?

_____

It's important to prioritize hearing God even when we're super busy. If God wants us to do something we should make sure to do it first, no matter how much we have going on. We need to be willing to adjust our schedules to make time for God.

I pray that each day you find it easier to follow God and the people in charge of you. Pray and thank God for helping you learn so much during this study. Ask Him to keep giving you wisdom and strength to use what you've learned in your everyday life.

COMPLETE WEEK 6 MEMORY VERSE WORK ON PAGE 72

EPhesians 6:1-3

Children, obey your parents in the Lord, for this is right. "Honor your father and mother"- which is the first commandment with a promise- "so that it may go well with you and that you may enjoy long life on the earth."

Day 1

_____

_____

_____

_____

_____

Day 2

_____

_____

_____

_____

_____

Day 3

_____

_____

_____

_____

_____

MEMORY VERSE WEEK 1

EPhesians 6:1-3

Children, obey your parents in the Lord, for this is right. "Honor your father and mother"- which is the first commandment with a promise- "so that it may go well with you and that you may enjoy long life on the earth."

Day 4

_____

_____

_____

_____

_____

Day 5

_____

_____

_____

_____

_____

At the end of day 5, repeat this week's memory verse to a parent by heart. Check off the heart when completed!

♡ ___EPhesians 6:1-3___

MEMORY VERSE WEEK 2

Philippians 2:14-16

"Do everything without grumbling or arguing, so that you may become blameless and pure, "children of God without fault in a warped and crooked generation." Then you will shine among them like stars in the sky..."

Day 6

_____

_____

_____

_____

_____

Day 7

_____

_____

_____

_____

_____

Day 8

_____

_____

_____

_____

_____

MEMORY VERSE WEEK 2

Philippians 2:14-16

"Do everything without grumbling or arguing, so that you may become blameless and pure, "children of God without fault in a warped and crooked generation." Then you will shine among them like stars in the sky..."

Day 9

_____
_____
_____
_____
_____

Day 10

_____
_____
_____
_____
_____

At the end of Day 10, repeat this week's and last week's memory verses to a parent by heart. Check off the hearts when completed!

♡ _Ephesians 6:1-3_

♡ _Philippians 2:14-16_

MEMORY VERSE WEEK 3

John 14:21

"Whoever has my commands and keeps them is the one who loves me. The one who loves me will be loved by my Father, and I too will love them and show myself to them."

Day 11

_____

_____

_____

_____

_____

Day 12

_____

_____

_____

_____

_____

Day 13

_____

_____

_____

_____

_____

John 14:21

"Whoever has my commands and keeps them is the one who loves me. The one who loves me will be loved by my Father, and I too will love them and show myself to them."

Day 14

_____

_____

_____

_____

_____

Day 15

_____

_____

_____

_____

_____

At the end of Day 15, repeat the memory verses from weeks 1, 2, and 3 to a parent by heart. Check off the hearts when completed!

♡ __Ephesians 6:1-3__   ♡ ___John 14:21___

♡ __Philippians 2:14-16__

MEMORY VERSE WEEK 4

1 John 5:2-3

"This is how we know that we love the children of God: by loving God and carrying out his commands. In fact, this is love for God: to keep his commands. And his commands are not burdensome..."

Day 16

_____

_____

_____

_____

_____

Day 17

_____

_____

_____

_____

_____

Day 18

_____

_____

_____

_____

MEMORY VERSE WEEK 4

1 John 5:2-3

"This is how we know that we love the children of God: by loving God and carrying out his commands. In fact, this is love for God: to keep his commands. And his commands are not burdensome..."

Day 19

_____

_____

_____

_____

Day 20

_____

_____

_____

_____

At the end of Day 20, repeat the memory verses from weeks 1, 2, 3, and 4 to a parent by heart. Check off the hearts when completed!

♡ __Ephesians 6:1-3__   ♡ __John 14:21__

♡ __Philippians 2:14-16__   ♡ __1 John 5:2-3__

James 1:22-24

"Do not merely listen to the word, and so deceive yourselves. Do what it says. Anyone who listens to the word but does not do what it says is like someone who looks at his face in a mirror and, after looking at himself, goes away and immediately forgets what he looks like."

Day 21

_____

_____

_____

_____

_____

_____

Day 22

_____

_____

_____

_____

_____

Day 23

_____

_____

_____

_____

_____

MEMORY VERSE WEEK 5

James 1:22-24

"Do not merely listen to the word, and so deceive yourselves. Do what it says. Anyone who listens to the word but does not do what it says is like someone who looks at his face in a mirror and, after looking at himself, goes away and immediately forgets what he looks like."

Day 24

_____

_____

_____

_____

_____

_____

Day 25

_____

_____

_____

_____

_____

_____

At the end of Day 25, repeat the memory verses from weeks 1,2,3,4, and 5 to a parent by heart. Check off the hearts when completed!

♡ Ephesians 6:1-3   ♡ John 14:21

♡ Philippians 2:14-16   ♡ 1 John 5:2-3

♡ James 1:22-24

MEMORY VERSE WEEK 6

Acts 5:29

"But Peter and the other apostles replied,
'We must obey God rather than men.' "

Day 26

_____

_____

_____

Day 27

_____

_____

_____

Day 28

_____

_____

_____

MEMORY VERSE WEEK 6

Acts 5:29

*"But Peter and the other apostles replied,
'We must obey God rather than men.' "*

Day 29

_____

_____

_____

Day 30

_____

_____

_____

At the end of Day 30, repeat the memory verses from all 6 weeks to a parent by heart. Check off the hearts when completed!

♡ __Ephesians 6:1-3__   ♡ __1 John 5:2-3__

♡ __Philippians 2:14-16__   ♡ __James 1:22-24__

♡ __John 14:21__   ♡ __Acts 5:29__

Made in the USA
Columbia, SC
07 June 2025